Animal Neighbours

Hare

Michael Leach

Hodder
Wayland

An imprint of Hodder Children's Books

Animal Neighbours

Titles in this series:
Badger • Deer • Fox • Hare • Hedgehog • Otter

Conceived and produced for Hodder Wayland by

Nutshell
MEDIA

Intergen House, 65-67 Western Road, Hove BN3 2JQ, UK
www.nutshellmedialtd.co.uk

Commissioning Editor: Vicky Brooker
Designer: Tim Mayer
Illustrator: Jackie Harland
Picture Research: Glass Onion Pictures

Published in Great Britain in 2003 by Hodder Wayland, an imprint of Hodder Children's Books.

British Library Cataloguing in Publication Data
Leach, Michael, 1954–
Hare. – (Animal neighbours)
1. Hares – Juvenile literature
I. Title
599.3'28

ISBN 0 7502 4170 5

Printed and bound in Hong Kong.

Hodder Children's Books
A division of Hodder Headline Limited
338 Euston Road, London NW1 3BH

Cover photograph: A brown hare listens for sounds of danger.
Title page: A male and female hare 'boxing'.

Picture acknowledgements
FLPA 17 (Richard Brooks), 24–25 (D. T. Grewcock); Michael Leach 16, 25, 27; naturepl.com *Cover* (Hanne
& Jens Erikesen), 6 (John Cancalosi), 11 (David Welling), 21 Herman Brehm), 26 (Brian Lightfoot);
NHPA *Title page*, 7, (Manfred Danegger), 9 (Andy Rouse), 10 (Manfred Danegger), 12 (Andy Rouse), 14,
15, 19, 20, 22, 23 (Manfred Danegger), 28 right (Andy Rouse), 28 bottom, 28 top left (Manfred
Danegger); Oxford Scientific Films 8, 13, 28 top (Gary & Terry Andrewartha/SAL).

Contents

Meet the Hare

Hares are small, fast mammals, with long ears, short tails and powerful hind legs. They live in fields and moorland, deserts and mountains. In North America, hares are called jackrabbits.

There are 22 species of hare alive today living throughout the world. This book looks at the brown hare, the most common and widespread species.

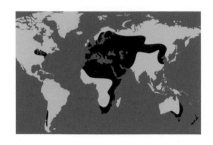

▲ **The red areas on this map show where brown hares live in the world today.**

Coat

The hare's yellow-brown coat is perfect camouflage when it crouches down and lies still on the soil.

Legs

The hare's long, strong back legs make it one of the fastest running animals.

Feet

Hares drum their feet on the ground to warn others that danger is nearby. They also use their strong feet to kick enemies.

Tail

A hare's tail has a thick, black stripe on top, very different to the snow-white tail of a rabbit.

▲ **The brown hare is slightly bigger than a domestic cat.**

Ears

Large ears allow the hare to hear enemies a long way away. The ears can move separately, and each can be aimed in different directions, so the hare can listen to sound coming from all around. Hare ears always have a black tip.

Eyes

The hare has eyes on the sides of its head. This allows it to look for danger in front and to both sides at the same time.

Nose

The hare has an excellent sense of smell. Its nostrils close when feeding on loose soil or in high winds, which stops dust blowing in and damaging the sensitive passages inside. This is known as winking.

Teeth

The hare's teeth are designed for chewing plants. Sharp incisors at the front of the mouth bite through stems. Behind these, large, flat teeth called premolars and molars are used for chewing.

◀ **The brown hare.**

HARE FACTS

The brown hare's scientific name is *Lepus europaeus*, from the Latin words *Lepus*, meaning 'hare' and *europaeus* meaning 'European'.

Fully grown hares measure about 55 cm long. Their ears are about 10 cm long. Hares weigh about 3.5 kg. Males and females are about the same size.

The Hare Family

Hares belong to a family known as the lagomorphs, which is made up of hares, pikas and rabbits. Pikas are small, shy creatures that live in the mountains of North America and the deserts of Asia. They spend all summer and autumn collecting leaves and grass, which they store underground. They will need this food throughout the winter months, when food disappears in these harsh, dry habitats.

The European rabbit is one of the world's most widespread mammals. Originally it was found only in southern Europe but over the past 2,000 years, rabbits have been deliberately introduced to many countries to be hunted for food. They are now found all over the world, including Australia, North America and Britain.

▼ The pika of North America is known as a whistling hare because it produces a high-pitched scream when it is frightened.

LAGOMORPHS

In the nineteenth century, Charles Darwin and other naturalists thought that hares and rabbits were related to rats and mice, and belonged to the rodent family. In 1912, scientists realised that they belonged to a separate family, and created the lagomorph family. Lagomorphs have an extra set of teeth that is missing in rodents. They also have very different digestive systems.

▲ While the rest of its coat turns white, the tips of the mountain hare's ears stay black.

Some species of hare are specially adapted to their habitat. The mountain hare's fur is brown in the summer, but in late autumn it grows a thick, white coat. This camouflages it from predators when snow covers the landscape. The antelope jackrabbit, which lives in the deserts of the USA, has very long ears. Apart from detecting predators, the ears also give off heat, which helps keep the hare cool.

Birth and Growing Up

When a pregnant female hare is ready to give birth, she digs a shallow dip in the earth, called a form. She will make sure the form is not far from the nearest feeding area, so she will not have far to travel to eat after giving birth.

Young hares are called leverets. They are born with their eyes open and with long, silky fur. Their hearing and sense of smell are also well developed. These early senses and fur are essential to young born out in the open, to help detect predators and keep warm.

LEVERETS

There are usually two or three leverets in a litter.

New-born leverets are about 8 cm long and weigh about 110 g.

For their first month, leverets grow at a rate of 35 g a day. They reach their full body weight at about 8 months.

▼ These leverets are just a few hours old.

▲ Each leveret keeps very still as it crouches in its form.

The leverets can walk immediately after birth, but they stay in the form for their first three days. After three days, each leveret finds its own hiding place, a few metres from the birth place. It is safer for the leverets to move apart from each other because it is harder for predators to spot individuals than a group. Each day at sunset, the leverets return to the birth place and suckle from their mother.

Early days

When they are about 3 weeks old, the leverets eat their first solid food. This is grass and other plants, which is the same food that adult hares eat. The leverets continue to suckle from their mother until they are about 6 weeks old, when she gives birth to her next litter.

As the leverets grow, they become very active and start to chase each other around. This is important exercise that strengthens their muscles for running and allows them to explore their surroundings.

▲ Two leverets suckle from their mother. Hare milk is very rich, which helps the leverets to grow quickly.

CROSS-SUCKLING

Leverets sometimes suckle from female hares that are not their mother. This is known as cross-suckling. It usually happens in areas with a high population of hares, where there are lots of females feeding young. Hungry leverets can mistake any small moving animal for a female hare. Sometimes they follow each other by mistake when they are looking for milk.

The first few months of the leverets' lives are extremely dangerous. They are hunted by a wide range of predators, including eagles, owls and foxes. About 50 per cent of leverets are killed before they reach the age of 6 months.

▼ With their excellent eyesight, golden eagles flying overhead can often spot leverets hiding on the ground below.

Habitat

Brown hares live in large, open habitats such as farmland and moorland. They particularly like grassy meadows and fields of cereal crops. Besides providing food, these areas allow the hares to spot enemies long before they get too close.

Hares avoid woodlands because not enough food plants grow on the dark woodland floor. Also, they do not like to be surrounded by trees and bushes, where predators can hide. In very bad weather, hares sometimes hide just inside the edge of woodland, but only to shelter from the wind or rain. They never move far from the food and safety of open fields.

▼ In a ploughed field, a crouching hare can be mistaken for a stone or a clump of soil.

HARE TRAVEL

Brown hares were once only found in Europe and Asia. But in the eighteenth and nineteenth centuries, European settlers introduced them to other parts of the world such as Australia, New Zealand, North and South America. They released live hares into the lands where they settled so they could continue hunting the hares and eating their meat.

▲ This hare is sheltering from the hot sun on the edge of a wood.

About 5,000 years ago, when most of Europe was covered in woodland and forest, hares were much rarer than they are today. As the forests were cut down to make more farmland, hare populations steadily grew. Over the last 100 years, the creation of even bigger fields suitable for farm machinery has provided perfect feeding and breeding grounds for hares.

Safety in numbers

Hares are not sociable animals. They sleep and feed alone, but they live close to each other for protection. A single hare cannot feed and keep a look out for predators at the same time. But between them, a group of ten hares can watch an entire field for signs of danger. If any one hare starts to run, all the hares in the group become instantly aware that a predator is approaching.

HIGH-SPEED HARE

The brown hare is one of the world's fastest mammals. When chased by enemies, an adult can reach speeds of up to 70 kph. Hares often escape predators by suddenly changing direction while running at full speed. Few hunters can turn this quickly.

▼ When one hare starts to run, every hare nearby will follow.

COMMUNICATION

Hares are mostly silent throughout their lives. They let other hares know of approaching danger simply by running. Females make a series of low, coughing grunts to call their young. The only other noise hares make is when they are extremely frightened, when they produce a low grunt or high-pitched scream.

▲ Two pairs of eyes, looking in different directions, can spot danger much quicker than just one pair.

Hares are nocturnal animals. They eat mainly at night, although during the summer in northern Europe, when nights are short, they also feed in the early morning and evening. Their days are spent resting. Hares seen moving around in the daylight have probably been disturbed by humans or animal predators.

15

Forms

Unlike most small mammals, hares do not dig
underground dens. They spend their lives above
ground, even when asleep. They rest in shallow dips
in the ground or vegetation, known as forms. On
moorland, the forms can simply be vegetation that is
flattened by the hare's body. In this habitat, where
the plants are thick and tall, hares are well-hidden
from enemies.

▲ Long grass makes
an excellent form for
a resting hare. The
hare keeps its ears
down flat to hide
from predators.

WHAT'S THE DIFFERENCE?

- Hares have black tips to their ears; rabbits do not.
- Hares have yellow-brown coats; rabbits have grey coats.
- From behind, a hare's tail looks black; a rabbit's tail looks white.
- Hares have long, visible legs; rabbits' legs are often hidden from view.
- Hares run like dogs and are much faster than rabbits; rabbits scamper around.
- Hares feed in the centre of large fields, well away from shelter; rabbits usually feed close to their warrens, in hedgerows or woodlands.

On farmland the vegetation is often short. So before going to sleep, hares dig a form into the soil. Then they crouch down low in it, with their ears folded flat along their backs. They close their eyes and do not move, becoming almost invisible. During the day, the field will look completely empty. At sunset, when the hares wake up, it can seem as if they suddenly appear from nowhere.

▼ **This hare has dug a form in the short stubble left when a crop has been harvested.**

Food

Hares are herbivores, which means they eat only plants. Their main food is grass, and cereal crops such as corn and barley, but the hare's diet changes throughout the year depending on the food available.

▼ **Leverets have more predators than adult hares because they cannot run as fast. (The illlustrations are not to scale.)**

Hare food chain

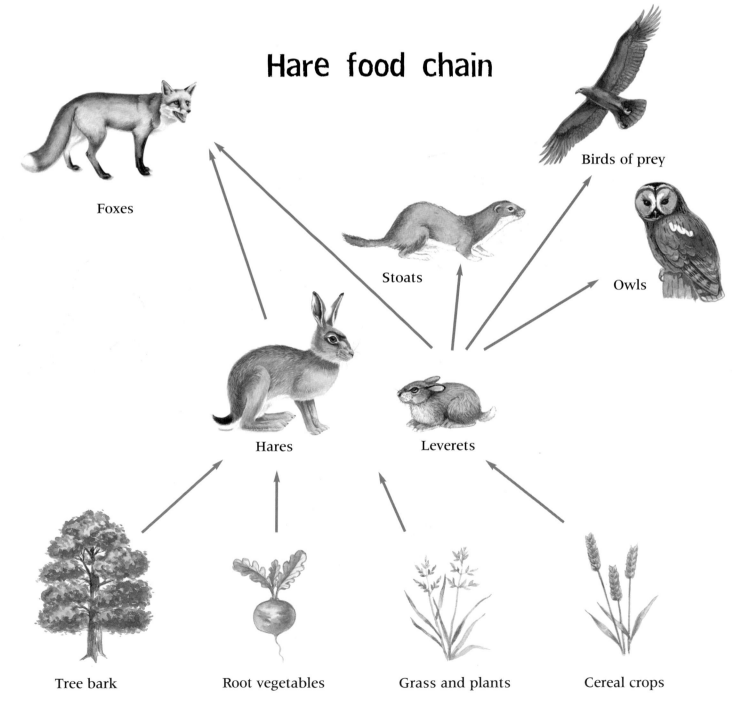

Foxes

Birds of prey

Stoats

Owls

Hares

Leverets

Tree bark

Root vegetables

Grass and plants

Cereal crops

TEETH

Plants are tough and hard to chew. Most animals have teeth that stop growing when they become adult, but the hare's sharp incisor teeth continue to grow throughout its life. Eating wears down the teeth at about the same rate as they grow, so the teeth stay the same size.

Food is easy to find in the spring and summer, when fields are full of tender young crops. By the end of the autumn, however, the best food has disappeared. The grass stops growing when winter arrives and many wild plants lose their leaves. Only winter wheat and a few other cereals remain in the fields. This is the time that hares start to eat turnips and other root crops that are still in the ground. They also use their sharp incisor teeth to strip and eat bark from trees.

▲ Hares stand on their hind legs to reach buds and leaves.

Digestion

Green plants contain a tough substance called cellulose. This is difficult to digest, so hares and other members of the lagomorph family have a special way of eating. They eat quickly throughout the night, trying to take in as much food as possible. At dawn, they return to their forms and rest.

During the day, hares produce soft, oval droppings containing food that has been softened, but only partly digested. They immediately eat the droppings so that the food passes through their digestive system for a second time. This allows the hare to absorb all the nutrients and vitamins from the food, in a process called refection. Finally, at night, hares produce hard, black droppings, which are not eaten.

◀ **In the summer and autumn, ripe farm crops such as maize provide a delicious feast.**

EATING AND LISTENING

Even while they are eating, hares are constantly on the alert for danger. As they munch on grass and cereal crops, their ears act as antennae, moving backwards and forwards, picking up any danger signs. At the first sound of danger, the hare will sprint for safety.

The hare's eyes are ▶ very good at spotting movement. At the first sign of danger, the hare will stop feeding immediately and sprint.

Finding a Mate

Hares breed between February and September every year. In February and March, male hares start to follow females around as they feed. Stronger males drive off any rivals that come near, running at them or biting them until the weaker hare runs off.

As a male tries to get closer to a female, she sometimes hits him with her front feet. This behaviour started the story of the 'mad March hare'. It was once thought that 'boxing' hares were fighting males, but we now know that it is a female trying to drive away a male.

▼ **Hare fights look very dramatic, but the animals are rarely injured.**

▲ Boxing may help female hares decide which male is strong enough to mate with.

HARE EGGS?

For centuries, people all over Europe believed that hares laid eggs. The open fields where leverets are born are shared with birds such as curlews and lapwings. In the spring, these birds lay their eggs in shallow scrapes on the ground, similar to the forms where leverets are born. When people found the nests, they thought they belonged to hares.

Eventually the female allows the male to approach and they mate. The male immediately begins to search for another female and plays no part in raising the young. The leverets are born 42 days after mating. Female hares have three or four litters a year, and they usually mate again shortly after giving birth.

Threats

Healthy adult hares run too fast to be caught by most predators. Foxes and other hunters can sprint quickly over short distances but they soon tire, whereas hares can run at high speed for a long time. It is usually just the young, weak or injured hares that are caught.

The red fox is the hare's ▶ most dangerous predator.

Over half of all leverets are killed and eaten within their first few weeks of life. Even when they become independent, leverets cannot move as fast as adults and are often caught by foxes, owls, buzzards or stoats.

Hares have always been hunted by humans, at first for food but more recently for sport. Fast dogs, such as greyhounds, are specially trained to chase and kill hares in a sport known as hare coursing. Some people feel this sport should be banned.

▼ Even greyhounds are not always fast enough to catch a running hare.

DEBATE

Hare coursing is a very old sport. Supporters claim that:

- The animals die quickly,
- Very few hares are killed,
- Hares are farm pests that need to be controlled.

People wanting to ban hare coursing argue that:

- Hares are becoming rare,
- Hunting with dogs is cruel,
- Hares do little damage to the countryside.

Modern farming

▲ This hare has been killed by a farm machine that makes straw bales.

Over 200 years ago, hares were a common sight over much of Europe, but today their populations are dropping. This is mainly because of changes in farming methods. Most farms in the past were mixed, which meant they grew crops and kept livestock. Modern farms mostly specialise in either crops or livestock, instead of a mixture of both.

On a crop farm, when the crops are harvested, the hare's cover is suddenly taken away. On livestock farms, there are no crops to hide amongst. Modern farms are also using more pesticides, which poison hares when they eat sprayed crops.

▲ This hare has been killed by a farm machine that makes straw bales.

LIFESPAN

Hares can live up to the age of 3 or 4 years in the wild, but most die before the age of 18 months. Very few hares reach their third birthday and none die of old age. The few that last longer than 4 years become slow and are soon caught by predators.

Farm machinery kills many young hares every year. When danger threatens, young hares crouch on the ground and stay very still. This is no defence against a tractor or combine harvester working in fields. After harvesting, farmers sometimes set fire to the remaining stalks. This is known as stubble burning and kills hundreds of hares every year.

▼ Stubble burning prepares fields for ploughing and replanting, but the moving wall of flames kills hares and many other animals that cannot escape in time.

Hare Life Cycle

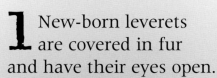

1 New-born leverets are covered in fur and have their eyes open.

2 For their first three days, the litter stays together. Then each leveret finds its own hiding place, a few metres away.

5 In the first spring after they were born, the hares start to breed.

4 At about 1 month old, the leverets are weaned.

3 The leverets suckle from their mother until they are about 3 weeks old, when they eat their first solid food.

Hare Clues

Look out for the following clues to help you find signs of a hare:

Footprints
Hare footprints are much bigger than a rabbit's. The back feet are wide apart and leave long, large prints showing five toes. The front feet are closer together, round and much smaller, with only four visible toes.

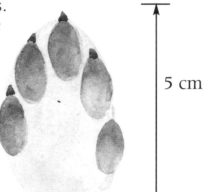

5 cm

Pathways
Hares often make pathways through fields, on their way to good feeding areas. These are very narrow and usually away from thick undergrowth.

Droppings
Hare droppings are paler than those of a rabbit, and they contain more undigested vegetation. Hares leave droppings scattered in the middle of large fields, whereas rabbit droppings are usually found close to a warren or other shelter.

1 cm

Feeding signs
Tree bark that has been nibbled up to 40 cm from the ground is a sign that hares have been feeding. If the bark is eaten higher up the tree, the marks will have been made by a deer.

Fur
Look for long, yellow-brown hairs caught on fences, bushes or twigs on the edge of fields.

Forms
Shallow dips in the vegetation or holes scraped in the soil may be forms. They are usually in the centre of fields. Look for a few yellow-brown hairs.

Glossary

camouflage The colour or pattern of an animal that helps it blend in with its surroundings and makes it difficult to see.

cellulose Part of a plant that is very difficult to digest.

digestive system The passage of food through the body as it breaks down so the body can absorb its energy.

dominant The largest, strongest animal of the group.

form A shallow dip in the ground or vegetation, where hares rest during the day.

habitat The area where an animal or plant naturally lives.

herbivore An animal that eats only plant food.

incisors Sharp teeth at the front of the mouth, used for cutting and slicing.

litter A group of young animals born at the same time from the same mother.

molars Large, flat teeth at the back of the mouth that are used for chewing and grinding.

naturalist A scientist who studies animals and plants.

nocturnal An animal that is active at night and sleeps during the day.

predator An animal that eats other animals.

premolars Large, flat teeth at the back of the mouth, just in front of the molars, used for chewing and grinding.

refection The animal practice of eating droppings to gain the most nutrients from food.

rodents Mammals with sharp incisor teeth used for gnawing. Rats, mice and squirrels are rodents.

stubble burning Burning the remaining stalks and leaves of a crop after it has been harvested.

suckle When a mother allows her young to drink milk from her teats.

weaned A young mammal is weaned when it stops taking milk from its mother and eats only solid food.

Finding Out More

Other books to read

Animals in Order: Rabbits, Pikas and Hares by Sara Swan Miller (Watts, 2002)

Animal Sanctuary by John Bryant (Open Gate Press, 1999)

Animal Young: Mammals by Rod Theodorou (Heinemann, 1999)

Classification: Animal Kingdom by Kate Whyman (Hodder Wayland, 2000)

The Giant Book of Creatures of the Night by Jim Pipe (Watts, 1998)

Life Cycles: Cats and Other Mammals by Sally Morgan (Belitha, 2001)

New Encyclopedia of Mammals by David Macdonald (OUP, 2001)

Reading About Mammals by Anna Claybourne (Watts, 1999)

The Wayland Book of Common British Mammals by Shirley Thompson (Hodder Wayland, 1998)

What's the Difference?: Mammals by Stephen Savage (Hodder Wayland, 1998)

Wild Britain: Meadows by R. & L. Spilsbury (Heinemann, 2001)

Organisations to contact

Countryside Foundation for Education
PO Box 8, Hebden Bridge HX7 5YJ
www.countrysidefoundation.org.uk
Training and teaching materials to help the understanding of the countryside and its problems.

English Nature
Northminster House, Peterborough, Cambridgeshire PE1 1UA
Tel. 01733 455100
www.englishnature.org.uk

The Mammal Society
15 Cloisters House, 8 Battersea Park Road, London SW8 4BG
www.mammal.org.uk
Promotes the study and conservation of British mammals.

Wildlife Watch
National Office, The Kiln, Waterside, Mather Road, Newark NG24 1WT
www.wildlifetrusts.org.uk
Junior branch of the Wildlife Trusts, a network of local Wildlife Trusts caring for nearly 2,500 nature reserves, from rugged coastline to urban wildlife havens, protecting a huge number of habitats and species.

Index

Page numbers in **bold** refer to a photograph or illustration.